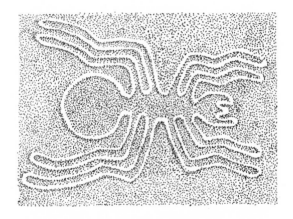

*The spider weaves the web of life, fate, and time and can also represent the sun with the web as rays of light. As a weaver of webs, and a lunar creature, the spider weaves the web of destiny at the center of the world and symbolizes the Fates. In Scandinavia these are the Norns, Urdh, Verdandi, and Skuld, who live at the foot of Yggdrasil, the World Tree, representing past, present, and future.*

First published in the United States of America in 2005 by
Walker Publishing Company, Inc.
Distributed to the trade by Holtzbrinck Publishers

For information about permission to reproduce selections from
this book, write to Permissions, Walker & Company,
104 Fifth Avenue, New York, New York 10011.

Library of Congress Cataloging-in-Publication Data
available upon request
ISBN 0-8027-1457-9
ISBN 13 978-0-8027-1457-2

Visit Walker & Company's Web site at www.walkerbooks.com

Printed in the United States of America

2  4  6  8  10  9  7  5  3  1

# WEAVING

## METHODS, PATTERNS, AND
## TRADITIONS OF THE OLDEST ART

written and illustrated by
*Christina Martin*

WOODEN
BOOKS

Walker & Company
New York

*This book is dedicated to Edith and Ron.*

*With thanks to the British Museum; the Victoria and Albert Museum; Lochcarron Weavers, Ross-shire; Carol and the spinners of Alston Hall; all the many skillful weavers and spinners I have met while researching this book; and the wonderful staff at Parbold Library for all their help.*

*The Loom of Dreams*

I broider the world upon a loom,
I broider with dreams my tapestry,
Here in a little lonely room
I am master of earth and sea,
And the planets come to me.

I broider my life into the frame,
I broider my love, thread upon thread;
The world goes by with its glory and shame,
Crowns are bartered and blood is shed:
I sit and broider my dreams instead.

And the only world is the world of my dreams,
And my weaving the only happiness;
For what is the world but what it seems?
And who knows but God, beyond our guess,
Sits weaving worlds out of loneliness?

*Arthur Symons*

# CONTENTS

# INTRODUCTION

Over time we have forgotten our link to the magic and mystery of weaving. The creation of clothing belongs to the material and metaphysical realms and in most traditional cultures is seen as a gift bestowed at the beginning of creation, often as an image of feminine power, related to the production of human life in the womb.

In the past, every inch of fabric was created from thread spun on hand spindles, an act of creation that we can only marvel at today. It is no wonder that garments were viewed as possessing great power. Those of a Maori chief could kill any man who wore them, while the Chinese still believe it is unlucky to walk under women's clothes left to dry. Cloth bestows metamorphosis (a Javanese magician wearing a magic sarong can transform into a tiger), and even today special clothes are worn to mark ceremonies unconnected with requirements of warmth and comfort.

The symbolism and folklore of spinning is rich and encompasses all nations and cultures. Plato's *Republic* presents the universe as a turning spindle with Earth at its center, and the planets placed at intervals outward on the whorl (*opposite*), a vision shared by the Kogi tribe of Colombia whose temples resemble spindles, which they see as a symbol of the cosmos. Their spun thread is their thoughts, and the sun turning around the world spins the Thread of Life.

People throughout time have seen weaving as central to their lives, a sacred act that is lost to us in these days of mass production, though clothing today still possesses its appeal in a secular form as we seek the latest fashions. I hope this book will connect the reader to the rich heritage of fibers, weaves, and fabrics and the folklore of their creation.

# FIBER
## *of mice and men*

Many fibers have been used through the ages for weaving. Sheep were domesticated in 9000 BC in southwest Asia, selective breeding producing wool of different lengths (called *staple*). Many lands grew wealthy on their wool trade, "Babylon" meant "Land of Wool." Seventeenth-century England protected its wool trade by making the wearing of cotton illegal, and shrouds were only to be made of wool.

The best wool belonged to the Moon God, god of shepherds, and shearing was done in June during a waxing moon. Shepherds were buried with a piece of sheepswool to explain at Judgment Day why they missed church. Other animal fibers used for weaving are soft cashmere from the Tibetan goat, silk, alpaca, angora rabbit, camel, and even dog hair.

Traditional vegetable fibers include cotton, used in India since 2700 BC, made from the hairy growth on the seed, and the blue-flowered flax plant, which along with hemp and jute produces its *bast fiber* beneath the surface of its stem. The Egyptians believed the gods created flax and their mummy cloth achieved a fineness of up to 540 linen threads per square inch. Moisture helps flax spin, so the fiber is often wetted, recalling the old woman with the huge lower lip in Grimm's *The Three Spinners*. Links to the feminine are seen in many countries' traditions, where women planted the seeds and performed high-kicking dances, even showing their genitals to the growing plants to encourage growth.

For mineral fibers Chinese scribes employed detachable asbestos sleeves that could be burned clean. Gold was spun as early as the Iron Age, and King Herod terrified onlookers with his godlike appearance in a spun-silver tunic.

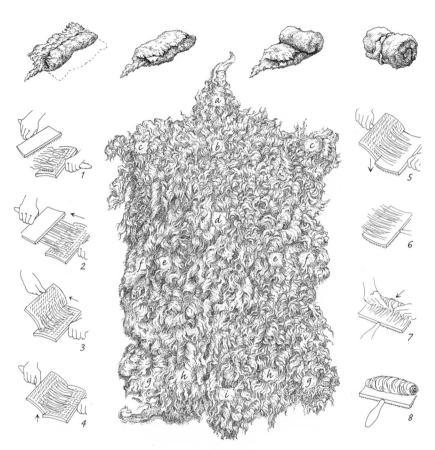

a. neck  b. shoulder  c. forelegs  d. back  e. sides  f. belly  g. hind legs  h. haunch  i. tail

The best wool in a fleece comes from the shoulder, then the back and sides; edges are poorest. Prepare the raw fleece by soaking overnight in warm water with a mild detergent, then rinse it without agitating the water, which would cause it to felt. It can now be carded as shown. Place wool on carder and brush it as in (1) and (2). Turn the carder around and transfer back onto the original (3). Repeat (1) and (2) until the fibers line up. Flip the right carder and lift the fibers off the left one as in (4), (5), and (6). Roll up to ready for spinning.

# SPINNING
## *a compound string theory*

Spinning takes short lengths of fiber, drawing and twisting them to create a continuous thread. The earliest method, dating back more than 10,000 years, uses a spindle, the stem made from wood or bone and the whorl from wood, clay, metal, or even a potato. Most yarn is spun counterclockwise, producing an S twist. Z twist yarn (spun clockwise) was used in rituals for healing, magic, and love charms.

Sometimes a distaff was used with the spindle to hold the fibers, usually flax. So we get the distaff side of the family and spindle kinship in medieval Germany. The term *spinster* originally merely referred to someone who spun, but by the seventeenth century it meant an unmarried woman. The spindle and distaff are universal symbols of feminine power, representing creativity and the continuance of life.

In many countries spinning stopped over Christmas and the distaff was bound with flowers to prevent its use, only recommencing after Twelfth Night on January 7th, St. Distaff's Day. St. Catherine was the patron saint of spinners, who stopped on her feast day, November 25th.

Jewish law says married women should not spin in public or by the light of the moon, and in Russia it was considered unlucky to lend a spindle. Couples wanting a baby girl put one under the mattress. Spindles were given to Japanese brides, and in other countries the father or fiancé would carve one for the bride. The spindle signified life.

Many goddesses related to the moon, such as Ishtar and Atargates, have spindles as attributes. The armless statue of the Venus de Milo is believed to have been spinning. Aphrodite spun rain from the clouds, and the Mayan Earthlord's daughters spun cotton into rain clouds.

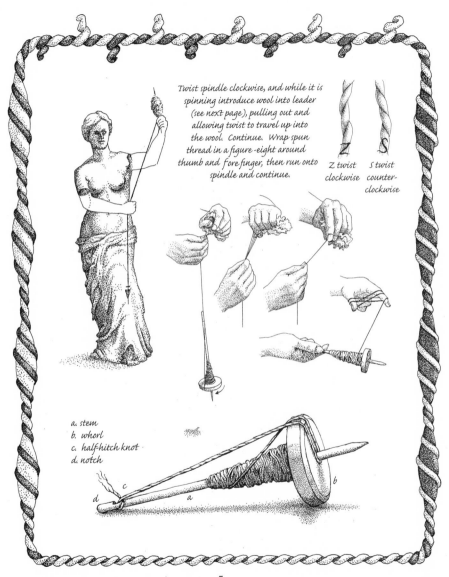

Twist spindle clockwise, and while it is spinning introduce wool into leader (see next page), pulling out and allowing twist to travel up into the wool. Continue. Wrap spun thread in a figure-eight around thumb and fore finger, then run onto spindle and continue.

Z twist clockwise

S twist counter-clockwise

a. stem
b. whorl
c. half-hitch knot
d. notch

# SPINNING WHEELS
## *thread from a circle*

The spinning wheel developed between AD 500 and 1000 through a number of stages, initially turning the vertical spindle horizontal and putting a groove in the whorl that could be driven by a band from a large, hand-turned wheel. In the sixteenth century, treadle power freed both hands, and a century later, spinning was seen as an accomplishment for genteel ladies. In India in 1920 Gandhi compared losing the wheel to losing a lung; he advocated spinning to create independence in his country, developing a portable wheel called a *charka*. Long before him, Aristophanes' Lysistrata had likened a statesman creating harmony in the state to a spinner drawing together tangled fleece to create yarn.

The classical Fates, Clotho, Lachesis, and Atropos, determined when life began and ended by spinning, measuring, and cutting the Thread of Life. Spinning also appears in many fairy tales – Sleeping Beauty pricked herself on a spindle, and Rumpelstiltskin spun straw into gold.

Thread is the very symbol of life. It was put on cattle, babies, and corpses to protect them from evil. A broken thread meant a quarrel, and it was unlucky to leave thread or the driving band on a wheel at night. Old Welsh sea captains would not allow wheels on board, and wool was not wound at night as it endangered seafarers. The Madonna is sometimes shown spinning, her destiny the redemption of the world.

maidens

driving
band

flyer

footman

mother
-of-all

table

wheel

treadle

1.

2.

3.

4.

5.

6.

*Opposite: threading a leader (prespun yarn), then splitting
it to introduce end of loose fleece.   This page: 1. grip leader
and fleece with right hand.  2. pull fleece out with left hand.
3. release right hand.  4. twist goes up pulled fleece.  5. grip
right hand where twist has reached.  6. move both hands
forward to allow thread to pull on bobbin.   Repeat 1-6.*

# DYEING
## *preserving the secrets of color*

The first Western dyers were probably the Swiss Lake Dwellers, around 3000 BC. All societies have guarded dyeing secrets, and in Anatolian society, a man would spend fifteen years learning to become a master dyer.

Dyestuffs called substantive dyes can be used straight on the wool, while adjective dyes require the use of a mordant (from *mordere*, to bite), which prepares the wool to accept the color. In the past, leaves, roots, and urine were used as mordants. In Pompeii, jars were left outside to collect urine, and dyers (known as men with blue fingernails) were consequently viewed with revulsion.

Colors can indicate status and bestow protection. In Greece saffron was a woman's color, used in puberty ceremonies. The first red dye is credited to blacksmiths, an imitation of the fire of the forge, and only they, and old men, were allowed to wear it. In India, Brahma, the god of fire and blacksmiths, has red cloth on his altars. The arsenic compound realgar produced a red dye, known as dragon's blood, which could make the wearer ill over time. So we see why Bronze Age myths said dragon's blood could kill. It is also possible that ancient Egyptians tried to dye live sheep, feeding them madder to produce red wool.

In Lebanon crushed shells of the purple murex mollusk litter ancient sites. Thousands were required to produce just one ounce of dye, its rarity making it a royal color. One legend credits Hercules' dog with the discovery, his nose becoming colored when he broke a shell. Pliny stated they should only be gathered at the rising of the star Sirius. In the Protoevangelium of James, the Virgin Mary is described as spinning purple thread for the Temple veil when the angel Gabriel came to her.

1. Mordanting prepares fibers for dyeing. The safest mordant is alum (potassium aluminum sulfate), 3 oz to 1 lb of wool, often used with cream of tartar. Others are iron (ferrous sulfate), tin (stannous chloride), chrome (potassium dichromate) and copper (copper sulfate). These are dissolved in water, and the prewetted yarn is added and simmered for 30 to 60 minutes. Copper-water mordant can be made by soaking copper in 50/50 water and vinegar for a week. Iron water is likewise made with rusty nails.

2. Dyeing: Use a stainless steel or enamel pan. Simmer dyestuff for 30 to 60 minutes (a few minutes only for berries) and strain. Many natural things can be used to color fiber, such as fresh flowers, roots, leaves, overripe berries, bark, green plants, and sawdust. Add wetted wool and simmer for 30 to 60 minutes.

# BASIC PRINCIPLES
## *the essentials of weaving*

Weaving is the interlacing of two sets of threads, normally set at right angles to one another, and is thought to have developed from basket making at least 10,000 years ago. The *warp* runs lengthwise and is held in tension, while the *weft*, or woof, passes over and under the warp. Warp and weft must link coherently, or the fabric will divide in two and not hang together. The device that holds the warp taut and separate is the loom. The way the threads interlace is known as a binding system, the three basic methods being plain weave, twill, and satin. The edges are made slightly stronger, and are called the selvage (self-edge).

Marriage is the weaving of opposites. The warp is usually finer, stronger, and is seen as masculine, while the weft is more supple and represents the feminine. Conjugal weaving is the union of male and female in intercourse, as believed by the Kogi tribe of northern Colombia, who also see the shaft and whorl of a spindle as the male and female reproductive organs. Seneca speaks of the coitus of warp and weft and in classical times a nuptial blanket covered lovers to signify their union.

Interweaving signifies the union of opposites, and weaving can function as a metaphor for many aspects of life. A writer weaves words to form verse or a tale, "spinning a yarn" to create a story, or intrigue. The words *text* and *textile* both derive from the Latin *texere*, to weave, and the Sanskrit word *sutra* (meaning thread) is a book formed of sutras as a fabric is of threads.

*Variations and developments of loom structures:*

*(1) single length, with shed stick (a) and leashes (b) to make alternate shed and countershed for weft insertion (often used for tapestry weaving).*

*(2) double length round pole with shed stick (a) and heddle rod (c).*

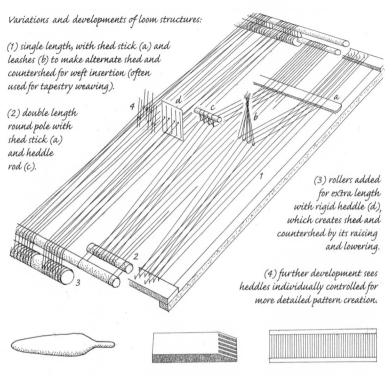

*(3) rollers added for extra length with rigid heddle (d), which creates shed and countershed by its raising and lowering.*

*(4) further development sees heddles individually controlled for more detailed pattern creation.*

*the weft is beaten down: a basic sword beater (above left), tapestry-style beater (above center), and a reed with twin function of warp separator and beater (above right).*

*Left: a warping frame, allowing long lengths of warp to be measured, every other thread forming a cross at top and bottom. Ties are applied at the ends and at intervals to stop threads getting confused. The warp is lifted off the frame as a chain to keep it from tangling (right).*

*Diagram on opposite page shows various shuttles: butterfly, stick, and thick card shuttle.*

# PLAITING
## *the earliest knots*

Plaiting, often known as braiding, is not strictly weaving, as the warp threads act in turn as weft. Plaited threads were used to make rudimentary clothing and for string nets. Dated 20,000 BC, the Venus of Lespugue wears an item known as a string skirt. In Homer's *Iliad* Hera wears a skirt with a hundred tassels to seduce Zeus, and until recently young women in Serbia wore an overskirt of threads to indicate their unmarried status. Navajo medicine men form their knowledge of the stars and planets into string games, akin to a cat's cradle.

In late-sixteenth-century France the art of producing braids and tassels was known as *passementerie*. In Japan the art is called *kumihimo* and was used in temples and for joining pieces of armor together, still later to fasten kimonos. Masters in specialist workshops taught the art's secrets.

Nowadays there is great interest in horsehair hitching, an intricate technique worked in a spiral around a core using half-hitch knots. Originally an eighth-century Spanish form, it was later developed in America, particularly by prisoners with time on their hands.

The use of human hair, which is practically indestructible, is documented back to Egypt and was very popular in Victorian Britain and America as sentimental jewelry in memory of a loved one. The hair was worked over a wooden core, boiled in water, then heated in an oven to set the braid. The work was often done by nuns and fashionable ladies working over a braiding table.

5-strand
3 to right, 2 to left; outside right over 2 to inside left, outside left over 2 to inside right.

5-strand
3 to left, 2 to right; outside left over 1, under 1 to inside right, outside right over 1, under 1 to inside left.

8-strand
strands arranged 3/1/3/1; under, over, under from the left, treating the 3 as 1.

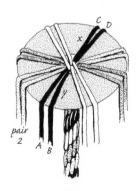

4-strand
2 to left, 2 to right; outside left behind 2 then over to inside left, outside right behind 2 to inside right.

card loom
16 strands, 4 colors; move A to x, move D to y, repeat with pair 2 and its opposite pair, repeat with each following pair, turning counterclockwise.

4-strand
tying white knot, then black knot, etc., with the knots in same direction each time, creates spiral.

13

# BRAIDING
## *slings and finger weaving*

Braids can be produced in a number of ways. Finger weaving is done without a loom, the threads attaching to a dowel and acting as warp and weft in sequence, as in plaiting. Prehistoric Andean and later Incan herders made ornate braided slings, which they used for guiding herds of alpaca, protecting crops, and hunting. In Viking times a tool known as a *lucet* (*below*), often made of wood, bone, or ivory, was used to make cords.

Around the Great Lakes the trading posts dealt in finger-woven sashes, particularly the *ceintures flechee* (arrow sash), or L'Assomption sash, made in that area of Canada and worn by the "voyageur." These were approximately six inches wide and twelve feet long, and could be wrapped around the body two or three times, and used as a pocket.

The inkle loom also produces braids. The loom uses true weaving, with a warp and weft, and its advantage over finger weaving is that it produces hard, firm braids with a warp-faced plain weave band. The width can be increased by sewing several together side by side.

The Asante people of Africa produce a strip-woven cloth called *kente*, originally made with raffia thread. The Asante believe that weaving was given to them by Ananse the spider, a wise and cunning figure in African folktales, and also a trickster. The *kente* has sacred and ceremonial meaning. The Hopi likewise make ceremonial sashes, the cloth depicting their experiences of eternity and relationship to the cosmos.

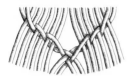

*twined braid*
*chevron, multiple colors,*
*16 strands, twine over pairs*
*to center using outer 2 from*
*left and right*

*now repeat for 2nd row;*
*pull tight, repeat; you can*
*twine rows clockwise then*
*counterclockwise*

*diagonal striped braid*

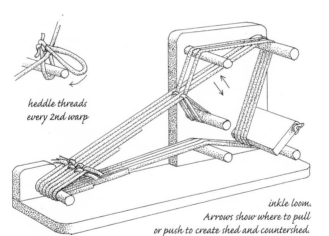

*heddle threads*
*every 2nd warp*

*inkle loom.*
*Arrows show where to pull*
*or push to create shed and countershed.*

*Threading chart; top row represents the open warp,*
*lower row the heddle warp, "x" marks white.*

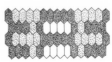

*pattern produced*

# PLAIN WEAVE
## *under over and over under*

Plain weave is the simplest weave structure, where the weft passes over one warp thread, then under one, creating a strong, durable fabric that is the same on both sides. Differences to this weave can be created using color, different yarns, different yarn thickness and spacing, tension, and yarn twist. Plain-weave cloth is suitable for printing and embroidery.

Little cloth survives from antiquity because of its perishable nature, but there are clay impressions of plain weave dating back to 7000 BC in Mesopotamia, and fragments of supplementary weft patterning have been found in the Swiss Lake dwellings dated 3000 BC.

In ancient Athens, women wove a rectangular woolen garment called a *peplos* to dress the statue of Athena at the Panathenaic festival on the Acropolis each year. The frieze of the Parthenon shows this ceremony. Woven in saffron and murex purple this garment showed the battle between the gods and the giants and was worked in supplementary weft on a warp-weighted loom (*see page 28*), giving a pictorial effect much like tapestry.

Plain weave is the basis of tapestry (*see page 32*), once imagined by the ancient Greeks as the medium of the starry sky, woven by Persephone. The Lady of Shalott likewise wove a tapestry reflection of the world she saw in her mirror, until, spying Lancelot there, she looked out of her window at him, and so brought about her demise. After her savage brutalization the Athenian princess Philomela depicted her story in tapestry, and the curtain of the temple of Jerusalem, torn at the death of Jesus, was an 80-foot-high Babylonian tapestry representing the cosmos.

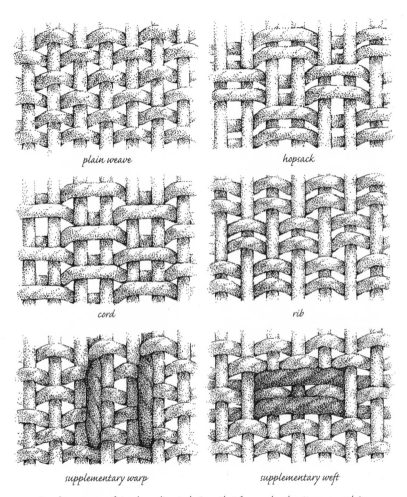

plain weave

hopsack

cord

rib

supplementary warp

supplementary weft

Supplementary weft is a brocading technique that forms colored patterns on a plain-weave background. Wefts can be continuous, from selvage to selvage, or discontinuous, where the cut ends hang at the back. In supplementary warp the additional warp threads are not essential to the structure of the fabric, but can add color or significance.

# TWILLS
## herringbone and denim

---

Twill weaves are softer, warmer, and resist wrinkling compared to plain weave. The earliest is dated 2600 BC, from Turkey. Twills are recognizable by their diagonal surface structure, the angle 45° being the most common. The structure is produced by crossing the weft over two threads of warp, then under two, across the fabric, then on the next row repeating this one-warp thread to the left or right. This is called $2/2$ twill. There is also the $3/1$ (over 3, under 1) and $1/3$ (over 1, under 3). $2/2$ twills have been found from the late Bronze Age in Scandinavia, produced on a warp-weighted loom. Wool workers, because wool is inclined to catch on itself, are credited with its first use in weaving because twills take the weft more easily than plain weave does.

The name *twill* is said to come from the French *touaille*. The Scottish tweed, a coarse twill, acquired its name when an invoice was misread in about 1840. Twills are either uneven, where the warp comes to the surface more or less than the weft, or balanced, where the warp and weft come to the surface equally. They are used for *denim*, the word believed to be a corruption of the French *serges de Nîmes*.

Cotton denim was first used to make overalls in the California gold rush. In 445 BC Herodotus described the cotton plant as a tree bearing fleece, called the wool-bearing tree. Later it was seen as a small lamb within the fruit pod. A packet of seeds sent to Georgia, in America, in the 1700s produced plants from which most cotton is descended.

2/2 direct

3/1 direct

1/3 direct

2/2 broken

chevron (herringbone)

2/2 reverse

*A minimum of three harnesses is required to create twill, though four is more usual.*
*The types of twill are: 1. The direct or straight twill, where the diagonal goes in a constant*
*direction left or right. 2. The pointed or waved twill, where the direction changes at even*
*intervals, includes herringbone and chevron effects. 3. The broken or reversed twill, which is*
*a satin where continuity is broken, said to be of Chinese origin.*

# TARTAN
## clan warpfare

Tartan, originally worn by Scottish Highlanders, now represents in all its brightly colored forms the national costume of Scotland. It is woven as twill whose pattern repeats in both warp and weft. The patterns were remembered by referring to threads tied around sticks and are usually symmetrical (*upper, below*) or, rarely, asymmetical (*lower, below*).

Cloth identical to tartan can be dated back to 1200 BC and found in the Tarim Basin mummies and the Hallstatt culture of Austria and Germany, which evolved into that of the Celts. The word as we recognize it was first used in 1538. Its Gaelic name *breacan* means checked.

Tartan was traded in England in the early eighteenth century, but after the battle of Culloden its wearing was banned. The repeal of the Act in 1782 brought a revival, and in 1842 the Sobieski Stuart brothers published a book of over 75 tartans, called *The Vestiarium Scoticum*. They claimed many were copied from a sixteenth-century document that then was lost, causing controversy over its authenticity ever since.

A person's name broadly dictates the tartan they may wear; or Jacobite or Caledonia can be worn as a general tartan. The bright Jacobite was originally worn in the eighteenth century as a secret sign of allegiance. Specific clans, districts, regiments, even countries, have a designated tartan, though the clergy is the only occupation to possess one (*opposite*). There is a Tartan Day, which is celebrated on April 6th in America and Canada, and on July 1st in the rest of the world.

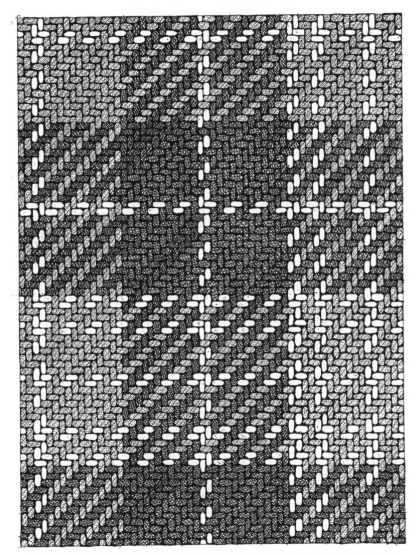

# SATIN
*smooth as*

---

In satin the warp threads float on the surface; when weft threads float it is known as sateen. These are glossy, soft fabrics whose threads are subject to snagging. It can be woven on a minimum of five shafts, the binding points moving left or right by at least two ends. It is usually woven face down to save lifting all but one shaft and stressing the warp.

Satin was originally made of silk obtainable only from China and takes its name from Zaytoun in the southeast. Silk's discovery is credited to the empress His Ling Shih, when a cocoon dropped in her tea and unraveled. It is the strongest natural fiber. The fabric passed along the Silk Road, named for it and the greatest trade route known, stretching from China to Rome.

Silk was worth its weight in gold, and how it was made was a closely guarded secret. Seneca thought it grew on trees, and Marcellinus said it was combed from the ground. Legend states that the secret was finally revealed in the sixth century AD when two monks smuggled cocoons out in hollowed walking sticks. In Japanese mythology, the goddess Ukemochi-No-Kami produced silkworms from her eyebrows. Many superstitions surround silkworms; in China they were not allowed to hear thunder or ever see lightning, a corpse, or a snake.

Damask, deriving its name from Damascus, alternates between satin and sateen weave to create ornate fabrics either in one color or using different colored warp and weft to create patterns. Damask from China often shows flowers or good luck symbols. Muslim men, forbidden traditionally to wear silk next to the skin, can wear a satin weave made of silk warp with cotton weft, called *mashru*, meaning "permitted."

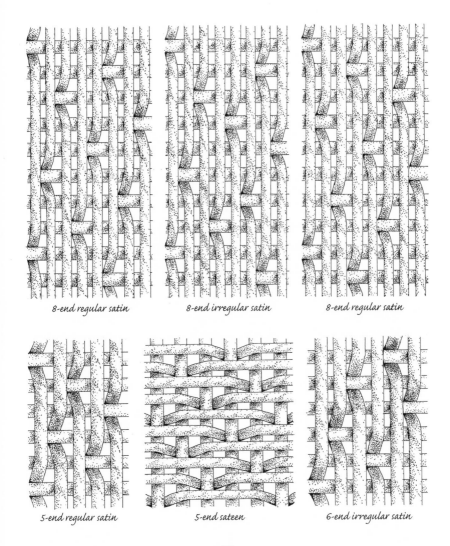

8-end regular satin

8-end irregular satin

8-end regular satin

5-end regular satin

5-end sateen

6-end irregular satin

# TABLET WEAVING
## *patterns appear*

Tablet weaving is believed to be the oldest form of pattern weaving, possibly dating back to the Bronze Age, and found in Egypt, Asia, Africa, and Scandinavia. This fascinating technique creates strong warp-faced bands of fabric often with intricate designs, such as lettering, and has been used to create ornate church vestments.

The tablets, usually square and also known as cards, have a hole in each corner, lettered clockwise A to D. In the past they were made of bone, wood, tortoiseshell, or horn, but they can be easily made from light card stock about four inches square. When rotated, either in unison or in groups, they raise and lower different warps to create patterns in the weave.

Using a number of tablets, say twenty, simple designs can be created with two colors such as black and white. To set up the tablet loom opposite, start by measuring out the warp threads, allowing extra length at each end, and arrange the tablets for threading. Next, following the threading diagram, thread black through holes A and B, and white through holes C and D, except for the two outer tablets, which are threaded with black only. Finally, tie one end of the warp to a fixed object and the other end to a piece of thick dowel (*p*), which itself needs to be fixed to something. Check and correct the warp tension.

Now, with AD to the top, and the tablets sitting on a surface, rotate all the cards one-quarter turn counterclockwise and insert a second dowel (*q*) about six inches from the first. Rotate all the cards another quarter turn clockwise and insert a third dowel (*r*) to ensure that the warp is held level and spread correctly. You are now ready to start weaving. Follow the instructions opposite.

By experimenting, many patterns can be created by this simple yet very versatile method.

24

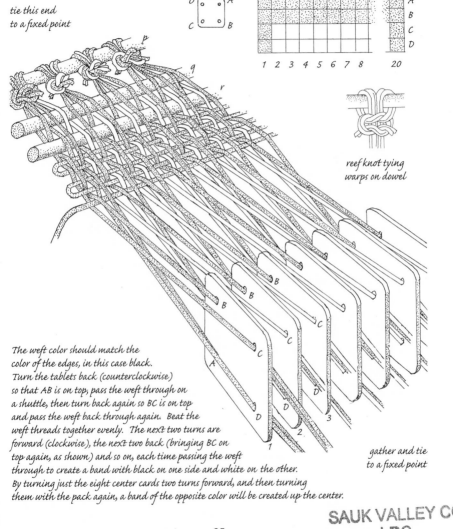

tie this end
to a fixed point

D A
C B

1 2 3 4 5 6 7 8    20

A
B
C
D

reef knot tying
warps on dowel

The weft color should match the
color of the edges, in this case black.
Turn the tablets back (counterclockwise)
so that AB is on top, pass the weft through on
a shuttle, then turn back again so BC is on top
and pass the weft back through again. Beat the
weft threads together evenly. The next two turns are
forward (clockwise), the next two back (bringing BC on
top again, as shown) and so on, each time passing the weft
through to create a band with black on one side and white on the other.
By turning just the eight center cards two turns forward, and then turning
them with the pack again, a band of the opposite color will be created up the center.

gather and tie
to a fixed point

25

# THE BACK-STRAP LOOM
## and the cloth of the moon and the sun

The back-strap loom is the most versatile and portable of looms, consisting of a number of sticks and a belt. The warp stretches between a fixed point and the weaver's body, which provides the tension. It is found in many areas, including Asia, China, Mexico, and Guatemala.

The Maya moon goddess Ix Chel is patroness of both childbirth and weaving and Mayan women have long worn a traditional blouse, called a *huipil*, which they have woven on back-strap looms since before the Spanish conquest. Spirits and gods, or nowadays saints, appear to them in dreams to inspire their depiction of the universe and the land of the Earthlord. The images on the huipil thus place the woman wearing it at the center of the Mayan universe. No two are identical, and their colors and designs also traditionally indicate the village of origin.

The design of the back-strap loom means the weaver is part of the loom. In northern Colombia, the Kogi tribe believes the loom is a symbol of both the human body and the topographical features of the Sierra Nevada. The Kogi temples possess four hearths and an opening at the top of the temple through which the sun can shine. At the summer solstice a beam of sunlight crosses the temple from the southwest hearth to the southeast hearth, weaving a thread of light by day and a black thread by night. Each day for six months the sunbeam moves slowly north, until, at the winter solstice, it crosses from the northwest to northeast hearth. The sun weaves the Fabric of Life on the loom that is the temple floor. It weaves two cloths a year, one for the sun and one for the moon, finishing at the equinoxes in March and September.

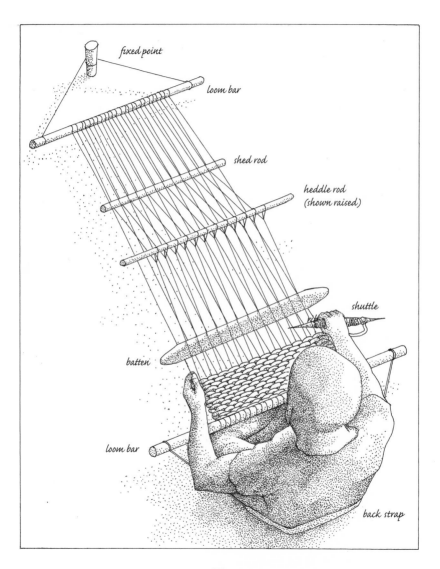

fixed point

loom bar

shed rod

heddle rod
(shown raised)

shuttle

batten

loom bar

back strap

# THE WARP-WEIGHTED LOOM
## an ancient technique

This loom is one of the oldest, dating back to 7000 BC at Catal Huyuk in Anatolia, and found also in Egypt, Scandinavia (where it is still in use), classical Greece, Rome, and among Native Americans. It produces plain weave, including tapestry, and twill weaves.

The warp threads hang from an upper beam, and the weaver must stand to work at the loom, beating the weft upward with a beater. In the past, warp weights were different shapes made of stone, fired clay, or lead. Aristotle compared stone weights with testicles, and the Orphics considered warp thread to represent semen. In the Icelandic saga of *Burnt Njal*, the Valkyries weave the fate of war on a bloody red loom, with men's entrails as warp and weft, and the heads of slain men as the warp weights.

The Chilkat Indians of southeastern Alaska use this style of loom, finger weaving by twining weft around the warp to create beautiful symmetrical patterns, which form clan crests. A Chilkat blanket was a prized and valuable possession, given as a mark of esteem or cremated with a dead chief.

In *The Odyssey*, Odysseus's wife, Penelope, used her weaving skills on this type of loom when her husband had been missing for twenty years and suitors were gathering. By her constant devotion she wove all day, insisting she must complete a shroud for her father-in-law, Laertes, before choosing a new husband, while secretly at night undoing all that she had done. It is for this reason that "Penelope's web" means something started but never finished.

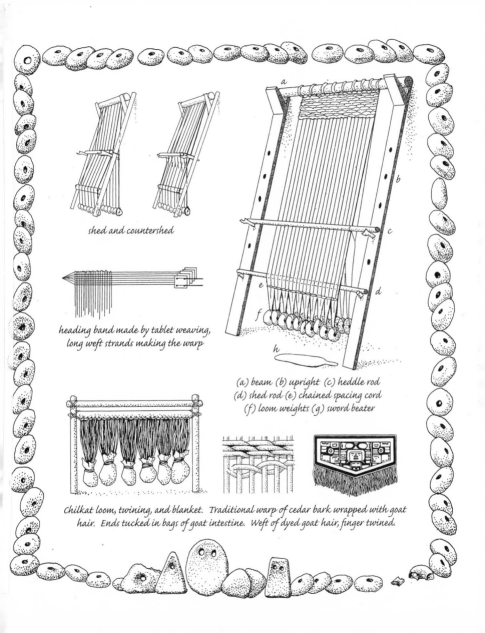

shed and countershed

heading band made by tablet weaving, long weft strands making the warp

(a) beam (b) upright (c) heddle rod
(d) shed rod (e) chained spacing cord
(f) loom weights (g) sword beater

Chilkat loom, twining, and blanket. Traditional warp of cedar bark wrapped with goat hair. Ends tucked in bags of goat intestine. Weft of dyed goat hair, finger twined.

# NAVAJO WEAVING
## *spiderman's sunbeams*

To the Navajo of Arizona weaving is a sacred art, with prayers and songs associated with every stage of the process. Their songs are passed from generation to generation, and baby girls have their fingers touched to spiders' webs to ensure their success as weavers.

Historically, weaving knowledge came from their neighbors the Pueblo, using cotton then wool from sheep introduced by the Spanish. Legend says that at the beginning of creation Spider Woman, living 800 feet up on Spider Rock in Canyon de Celly, taught the Navajo to weave. Her husband Spider Man (not the comic-book hero) provided the loom created from sky and Earth cords, with warp and weft of sunlight.

The traditional designs are geometric, sometimes brightly colored, as in the Eye Dazzler style, influenced by American Germantown yarns imported in 1880. The weavings possess hidden power in their asymmetric abstract patterns, bestowing protection, strength, and healing. In the past, blankets were smoothed by running them over a piece of sandstone, and some fabric was so fine it would repel water.

Since about 1920 the Navajo ceremonial sand paintings have been turned into weavings, though these involve the weaver in ritual incantations to protect him or her from harm. Alterations are deliberately woven in for the same reason. Sometimes objects are hidden in the weave, such as feathers in a saddle blanket for speed and animal sinew for endurance. A thread called a spirit line would often be woven in from the center to the border to allow the weaver's creativity out. It was believed that for good fortune, a weaver should not complete a blanket in one day.

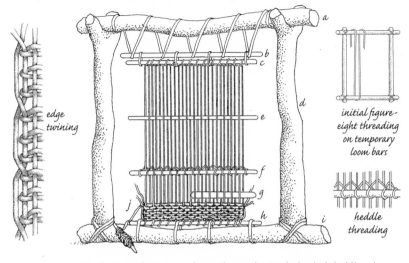

edge twining

initial figure-eight threading on temporary loom bars

heddle threading

(a) upper crosspiece (b) tension bar (c) warp beam (d) uprights (e) shed rod (f) heddle rod
(g) batten (h) web beam (i) lower cross piece (j) side cords for edge twining

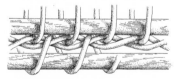

Loom bars stretch the warp, which is edge twined to space the warps. A cord ties this to the web beam. The loom bar is removed.

Navajo sometimes use wedge weave, which creates scalloped edges. Worked in one direction, then the other, chevron patterns are created. Weft is pushed down to cover warp.

# TAPESTRY
## *plainly woven pictures*

Tapestry weaving dates back to ancient Egypt and is a method of weaving patterns or pictures using plain weave so the weft covers the warp (*see below*), the weft being placed in small sections, not selvage to selvage. It can be worked on many different looms. Various methods for joining two areas, or colors, are shown opposite.

In the Middle Ages in France, Holland, Spain, and Italy tapestry reached its peak as a mural art and was used in convents, churches, and castles to provide warmth. The word originates from *tapis*, French for carpet. Notable tapestries were produced by large studios (*see title page*) and later designed by artists, creating ornate woven surfaces like paintings.

A full-sized drawing, or cartoon, is transferred with chalk or ink onto the warp, which must be strong and is traditionally of wool. The design is worked sideways so the tapestry hangs finally from its weft threads, which give it strength. The picture is worked from the back, using a mirror to view the front. Linen was used to create the whites of eyes.

The tapestry technique has also long been used in Asia, Peru, and America to create items other than wall hangings. One type of rug known as a kilim (from the Arabic *kalim,* meaning carpet) uses a tapestry technique. A kilim is made of stepped diagonal patterns characterized by short vertical slits appearing where two colors meet on adjacent warps. They are double sided and flexible and were also used as bed coverings or door hangings. The original magic carpet was probably a kilim.

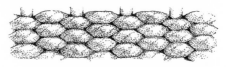

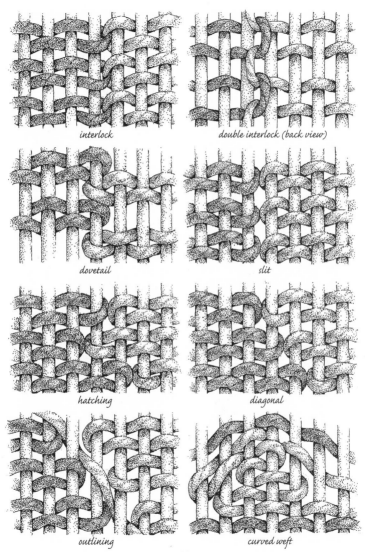

*interlock*

*double interlock (back view)*

*dovetail*

*slit*

*hatching*

*diagonal*

*outlining*

*curved weft*

# THE HORIZONTAL LOOM
*also known as the ground loom*

---

This loom was in use in Catal Huyuk in 6000 BC and is still employed by Bedouin tribes for its ease of use. It is worked lying flat on the ground and can be unpegged and rolled up as tribes move on. The maximum width of fabric produced on a horizontal loom is about three and a half feet, and the Egyptians used it to weave the finest linen prior to their use of the vertical loom. Fine knotted rugs can also be created on it and rich designs made by the use of pattern sticks, which lift the warps.

It was on this type of loom that Delilah wove seven locks of Samson's hair, to trap him while he slept. When his enemies came, he pulled the loom from the ground with his great strength, and it was only when she shaved his hair off that he was defeated. Hair possesses great power. In Malory's *Le Morte d'Arthur*, Dindraine, who lives a chaste life, weaves a girdle from her own hair for Galahad to wear to carry Solomon's sword.

Like Samson, Hercules was enslaved by a woman, Omphale the queen of Libya. She forced him to wear women's clothes and made him weave and spin. Hercules also traveled with Jason and the Argonauts in their quest for the Golden Fleece, which hung in the grove of Mars in the kingdom of Colchis, guarded by a sleepless dragon.

In the myth of Amor and Psyche, Psyche is given the task of collecting golden wool from vicious rams. Advised by a reed, she waits until they sleep and then by the light of the moon collects wool left on twigs. The ram also denotes the astrological sign of Aries, ruled by Mars, marking the spring equinox, when night and day are equal. Fleece has been endowed with power since Mesopotamian times, used in religious rites, as a cure, and possibly for collecting gold dust from running streams.

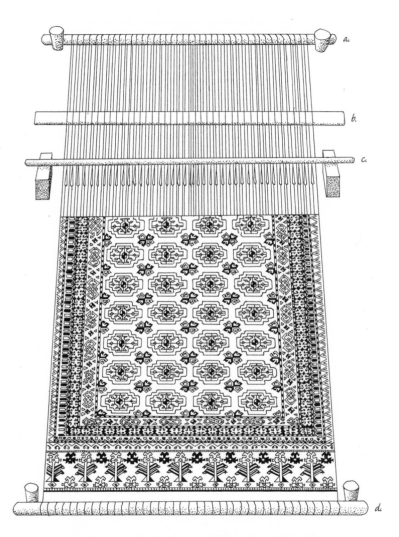

*a.* warp beam   *b.* shed stick   *c.* heddle stick   *d.* breast beam

# RUGS AND KNOTS
## *loose ends and warm, fluffy softness*

The oldest rug known is the ornately decorated Pazyryk rug, found frozen in a grave in Siberia and estimated to be 2,500 years old. It is now in the Hermitage Museum in St. Petersburg. This rug used the *Ghiordes*, or Turkish, knot, which creates strong, firm rugs. The other main knotting technique is the *Sehna*, or Persian, knot which gives a flexible pile. Both are named after weaving regions.

Many rugs use cotton as a warp, for its smoothness and resistance to stretching, with a weft of sheep's wool, goat or camel hair, or luxurious silk. In India, silk rugs could contain up to 2,000 knots per square inch. Spain was the first Western country to learn these Eastern techniques, which then spread to Portugal, England, and France. The Spanish used a knot worked on a single warp, called the Spanish knot. All these knotting techniques are then held in place by two or three rows of plain weave before another row of knotting.

In Scandinavia, *rya* rugs were produced using a version of the Ghiordes knot to create a double-sided pile fabric. Due to their warmth the rugs were used by fishermen and as a bedcovering. Brides had them as a part of their dowry and were married standing on them.

In the tale *A Thousand and One Nights* a seemingly worthless rug, simply by the power of wishing, becomes a magical flying carpet, able to transport the wisher. In another tale, a weaver beats all other craftsmen and is honored as the sheikh of sheikhs because he is able to teach a prince his trade in an hour. Islamic tradition says Solomon had a carpet that could transport him and his men.

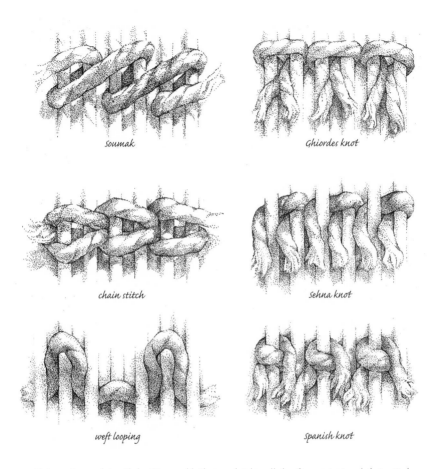

*soumak*

*Ghiordes knot*

*chain stitch*

*Sehna knot*

*weft looping*

*Spanish knot*

Flat weaving predates pile knotting, and both soumak (also called weft wrapping) and chain stitch can create pattern and texture. Weft looping has been found dating to 2000 BC and can create loop-pattern areas on a plain-weave background. Pile knotting creates soft, durable fabric particularly suitable for floor covering. A weaver might complete 10,000 to 15,000 knots a day. Designs are created by the placing of different colored knots, often worked to traditional patterns. The ends are either cut as they are worked, or the whole rug is trimmed upon its completion.

# RUGS AND SYMBOLISM
## *flying your magic carpet*

Oriental rugs are a microcosm within the macrocosm, consisting of an inner, seemingly infinite field surrounded by an outer border divided into multiple stripes. They are woven on the simple horizontal or vertical looms and can take months or years to complete. Each rug possesses an imperfection in its symmetrical lines or pattern, as only Allah can be perfect.

Arab tribes use these carpets to create a personal space during their nomadic wanderings and to protect them from evil. Blue beads or shells along a rug's edges protect the weaver from envy, while long threads extending from the edges allow evil spirits to leave. A rosette surrounded by two elongated leaves is often interpreted as the world surrounded by water around which two fish swim to create day and night and the seasons. The *boteh*, or almond nut, also known as the paisley pine for its use on shawls, is a common pattern on rugs. Its shape can be traced back to Babylon, where it represented the growing shoot of a date palm and from that came to be regarded as the Tree of Life.

Prayer rugs protect the devout Muslim from the ground and are recognized by the arch at one end, which is the *mihrab*, or prayer niche. This is oriented toward Mecca for the five daily prayers. The Lady Fatima, daughter of Mohammed, was a weaver of knots, and her hand is sometimes seen on rugs.

Chinese rugs were produced in organized workshops, incorporating many Taoist and Buddhist symbols, such as the lotus, the flute, and the fan. The Tibetans produced unusual tiger rugs, used to act as guardians and to indicate status.

# WEAVING DRAFTS
*coding for patterns*

Weaving drafts are the patterns that a weaver follows to create a fabric on a loom with two, four, or more shafts. They simply show where warp ends are passed through one of the heddles on one of the four shafts. A heddle is a wire with an eye at the center through which the warp passes. Each shaft is connected to a pedal, or sometimes to more than one. When that pedal is operated those shafts sink (or rise on the countermarch and jack looms) and the weft can then be passed through.

As weaving progresses and the fabric is cut off the loom, the weaver may be reminded of the stages of life leading to death. The warp represents the constant forces of the world while the weft passing back and forth recalls the transient affairs of man. The warp also represents the active masculine and the direct light of the sun, while the weft sings of the passive feminine and the reflected light of the moon.

The Dogon people of Africa believe their ancestor spirit gave them weaving by pulling threads between his sharpened teeth. The opening of his mouth gave the shed to weave through, and the threads also bestowed the power of speech. Weaving was not permitted at night because it was believed to weave silence and darkness into the cloth.

In Chinese legend the weaver girl (the star Vega) fell in love with the cowherd (the star Altair) and they had two children. But the jealous celestial queen mother separated them, running her hairpin across the sky to form the Milky Way, called the Silver River by the Chinese. On the seventh day of the seventh moon, magpies form a bridge so the two lovers can meet. In Japan this is celebrated in the Tanabata festival.

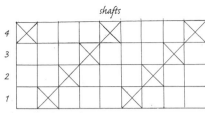

a. threading order

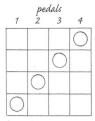

pedals
1   2   3   4

b. tie up

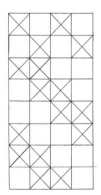

c. shedding plan

d. draw down

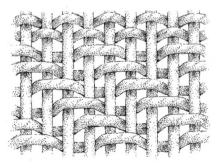

e. actual cloth

The draft consists of four elements:

a. the threading order - shows which shaft heddle the warp is passing through, seen from above, numbered 1-4 front to back.

b. the tie-up - shows which pedal connects to which shaft. A pedal can operate more than one shaft at a time.

c. the shedding plan - shows the order the pedals are pressed to create the pattern.

d. the draw-down - diagram of the finished cloth, in this case two rows of plain weave followed by a 2/2 twill (e).

# TABLE AND TREADLE LOOMS
## of heddles, treadles, shafts, and shuttles

The basic processes involved in using a rigid heddle, table, or treadle loom are the same, as the looms differ only in size and strength. On all three the warping takes time, but the cloth rollers mean that long lengths or several items can be woven each time.

The rigid heddle loom is the simplest, producing plain weave. The rigid heddle, traditionally carved from bone, wood, or ivory, spaces the warp and does the shedding and beating.

Table looms can have two, four, or more shafts, and the sheds are produced by levers, working on the same principle as the treadle loom. Table looms are operated by hand, whereas floor looms, having treadles, are operated by hand and foot and are therefore faster. They appeared in China possibly around 2000 BC and in Europe 3,000 years later. In thirteenth-century Europe strict regulations governed the length, width, and weight of cloth, and the two-man loom was introduced in Flanders to produce wider cloth.

Taoist doctrine states that the movement of the shuttle to and fro represents the alternation between life and death on the cosmic loom. The movement is also seen as a metaphor for copulation. Malay folklore tells of a cloth that weaves itself, each year adding a thread of pearls. When it is finished the world will end.

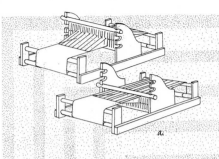

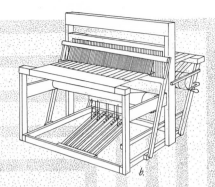

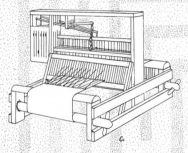

a. rigid heddle loom
b. jack loom - rising shed, harnesses work independently
c. table loom
d. counterbalance loom - sinking shed, harnesses work in tandem
e. countermarch loom - rising shed with more complex tie mechanism, producing a clear shed

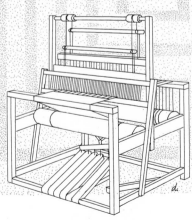

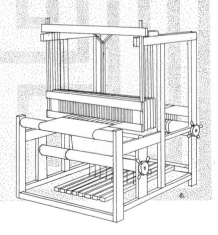

# THE DRAW LOOM
## and Jacquard loom

The draw loom enables ornate patterns more complex than those produced on a heddle loom to be woven. Originally, each warp was attached to a cord and individually lifted by an assistant, or drawboy, at the top of the loom. The master weaver threw the shuttle, in a process called "pulling the flowers." The draw loom originated in China, and its invention possibly dates back to 400 BC. Its use traveled west, so all European Renaissance—and baroque-pattern weaves were created on a version of this loom. It was used in Europe until the end of the eighteenth century.

In 1806, Joseph-Marie Jacquard in Lyons, France, invented a loom operated by punched cards to lift the warps in sequence. The loom was fast and could produce complex patterns, often resembling ornate medieval tapestries. French weavers greeted this development with hostility, and Jacquard died in poverty in 1834; but the idea was revolutionary (it directly influenced Charles Babbage in his early computer designs, as it was the earliest use of an information storage system). The complex loom enabled such items as shawls to be produced quickly and cheaply. Previously, Kashmir shawls were imported at great expense. Napoleon's wife, Josephine, owned hundreds of these original shawls and is said to have initiated their popularity.

Today these looms have themselves been computerized for even faster and more complex fabric production—a long way from traditional weaving skills, which, passed from mother to daughter, later guaranteed the girl wealth and a husband. Gone too today are many of the initiatory aspects of the art; perhaps no bad thing—in Venezuela girls were kept in solitary confinement for years while they learned to weave.

# ORNAMENTAL WEAVES
## *lacy gauzes and interlinks*

---

Gauze weaves create lacy fabrics, usually an open-work design made with plain weave. If gauze is combined with other weaves it is known as *leno*. Gauzes differ from other weaves, as the warp is active, crossing itself in areas and then being fixed in place by the weft. Gauze was used in Egypt as early as 2000 BC, and also in Peru and China.

*Sprang*, an interlinking technique, creates fine, open, elastic patterns but is actually a form of plaiting as it is created only of warp. The name comes from the old Swedish word, *sprangning*, and dates back to 1400 BC. The warp is twisted around itself from one end, creating a mirror image at the other, and is finally fixed in place at the center. It is worked on a frame with the threads under tension, and shortens by 15 to 30 percent when it is finished.

Twining, first used in basket making in Anatolia, dates back to at least 6500 BC. No shedding device is required in this technique as it is worked on a passive warp. The Maori create ornate geometric patterns called *taniko* using single- or double-pair twining. Their most valuable cloaks were sometimes given names and went on to become famous. Their legends tell of how a fairy was tricked by a group of women into weaving in the daytime so they could learn her skills.

The Maori also added feathers to create ornate rain capes, while Aztec rulers kept birds captive to supply their weavers, using white chicken feathers for weddings. Japanese folklore tells of the Crane Wife, who weaves beautiful cloth. Her husband spys on her to find out how she produces it, only to discover she is a crane weaving from her own plucked feathers. Once her secret is known she flies away.

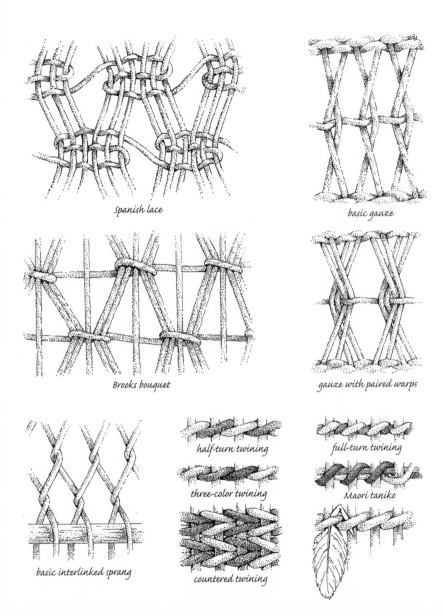

*spanish lace*

*basic gauze*

*Brooks bouquet*

*gauze with paired warps*

*basic interlinked sprang*

*half-turn twining*

*full-turn twining*

*three-color twining*

*Maori taniko*

*countered twining*

# FINISHING AND FRINGES
*all things come to an end*

---

Fringes have been used from Neolithic times to finish off a fabric, to prevent the weft unraveling, and to provide a decorative border. If the fabric has not been woven with four selvages, as in Navajo weaving, then various fringe, tassel, or stitching techniques can be used.

The Maori decorated their cloaks with tassels of white dog hair. The dogs slept indoors to keep their coats clean and were then occasionally shaved to provide hair for several cloaks. Some Native American men wore the fringe of their finger-woven sashes hanging to the left or right, to show their marital status. In Indonesia, a circular cloth was made continuously around a loom, with a gap left in the weft where the fringes would be. This cloth was left intact, the fringes cut only at important ritual ceremonies. These fringes were then dipped into a sacred spring, and the water was sprinkled onto the celebrant.

The Batak people of Sumatra create a sacred circular cloth called a *hijo marsitogutoguan*, with the fringe left uncut. The cloth ensures continuity of life from mother to child. It acts as a protector to various generations, its power gaining with time. Starting at one side of the uncut fringe the cloth represents the growth of the child through life until the other side of the uncut fringe is reached, representing a new generation beginning. Other Batak groups used an uncut circular cloth to encircle a couple at their marriage ceremony, to honor the union.

Weaving, an act of creation from the very dawn of prehistory, a gift given to all cultures by their gods, retains its power to intrigue and delight. We can still discover the joy of following the path from tangled fiber, to thread, to woven fabric, as generations before have done.

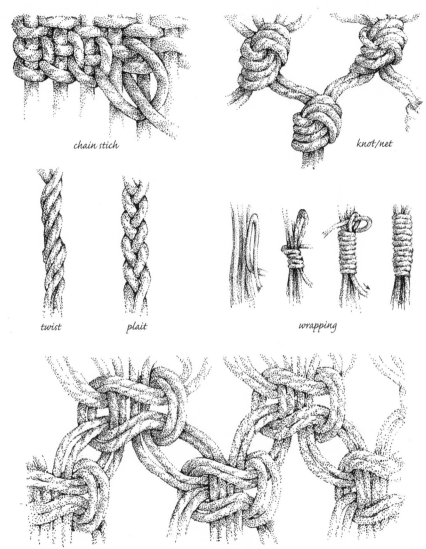

*chain stich*

*knot/net*

*twist*

*plait*

*wrapping*

*square knot*

# Simple Looms

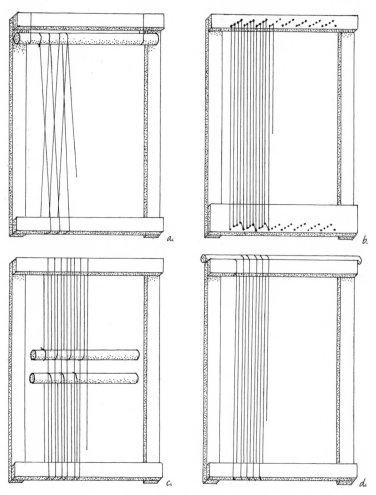

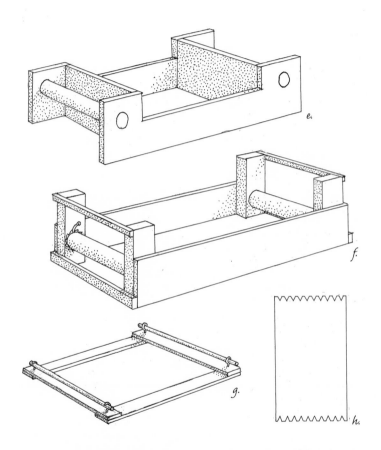

*(a), (b), and (g) are single-length frame looms. (c) and (d) are double-length frame looms.*
*(a) figure-eight with tension bar. (b) looped over nails. (c) two tension sticks at back.*
*(d) top tension bar can be removed as warp tightens.*
*(e) and (f) are roller looms. (h) is a card loom.*

# OLD ENGLISH LOOM

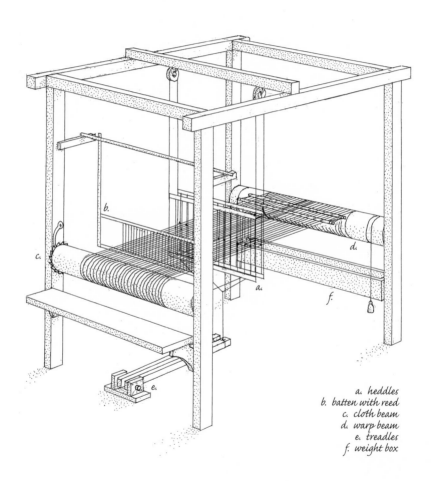

a. heddles
b. batten with reed
c. cloth beam
d. warp beam
e. treadles
f. weight box

# Floor Loom

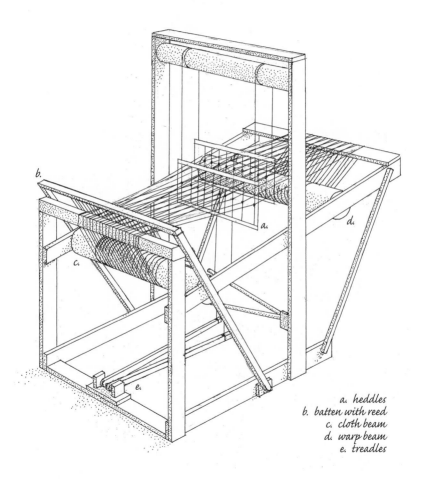

a. heddles
b. batten with reed
c. cloth beam
d. warp beam
e. treadles

# VARIATIONS ON PLAIN WEAVE

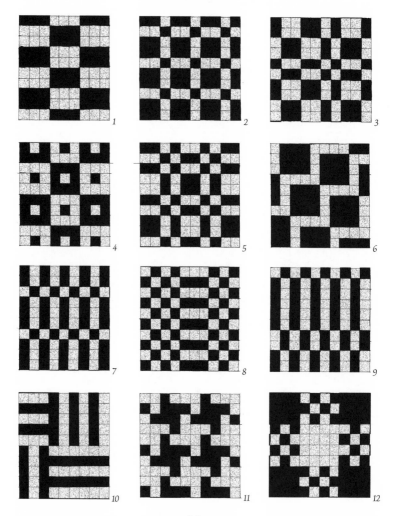

# VARIATIONS ON TWILL

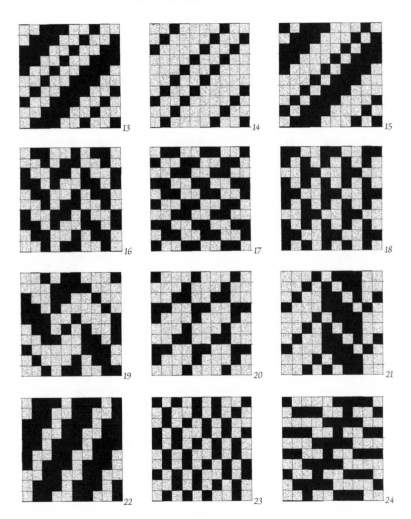

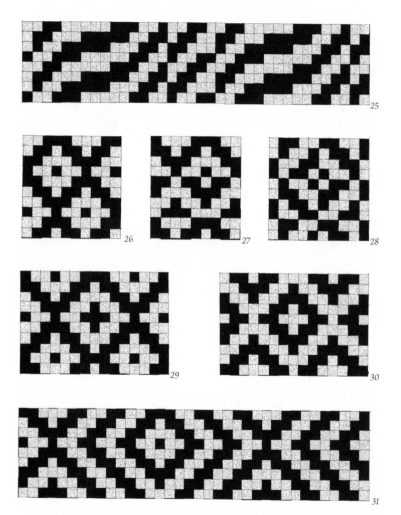

# COLOR EFFECTS

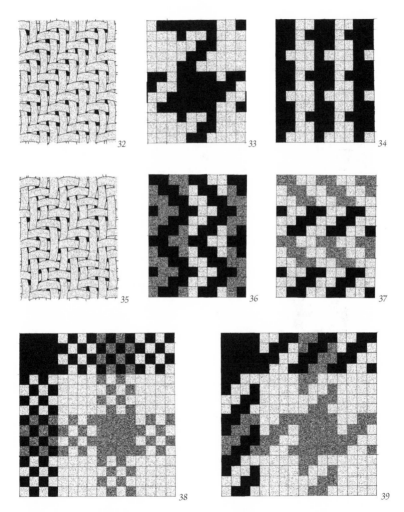

# GLOSSARY

*Bast fiber*—a plant whose fiber is beneath the surface of the stem for example, flax, hemp, and jute.

*Brocade*—cloth with patterns woven in with separate shuttles.

*Carding*—the preparation of fiber that combs them ready for spinning.

*Cloth beam*—on a loom, a front roller that holds the cloth.

*Damask*—cloth in which warp-and weft-faced satins alternate.

*Distaff*—a pole used to hold prepared flax for spinning.

*Float*—a short length of thread passing over two or more threads.

*Heddle*—a string or wire loop through which the warp threads pass, and which can then be raised or lowered to create a shed.

*Loom*—any device that holds the warp in position for weaving.

*Mordant*—a substance used with a dyestuff to aid absorption of the color.

*Reed*—a comblike piece of equipment used to separate the warp and beat down the weft.

*Satin*—a warp-faced weave with no definite diagonal lines.

*Selvage*—the firm edge of a fabric.

*Shed*—space between two layers of warp where the shuttle passes.

*Shed stick*—a flat stick used for opening the warp, creating the shed.

*Shuttle*—a tool for carrying the weft through the warp.

*Spindle*—a tool used to twist fiber into thread.

*Tapestry*—a weft-faced weave used for creating patterns and pictures.

*Treadle*—levers under the loom that raise and lower the heddle shafts, operated by the feet.

*Warp beam*—the roller at the back of the loom on which the warp is wound.

*Warp*—threads that run the length of the fabric.

*Warping frame*—a board on which a long warp can be measured out.

*Weavers knot*—a knot used to join two threads, a broken warp for example. Produces a small knot that can pass through the heddles.

*Weft*—threads that cross the width of the fabric.

*Whorl*—on a spindle, the weight at the top or bottom that helps it keep turning.

*Woof*—old name for the weft.

## KEY TO DIAGRAMS ON PAGES 54-57

*1-6: Basket weaves. 7-9: Rib weaves. 10: Log cabin, threaded D(dark), L(light), D, L, D, L, L, D, L, D, L, D, repeated in warp and weft. 11: Shepherd's check, threaded 2L, 2D, in warp and weft. 12: Check, 4L, 4D, warp and weft. 13-21: Twill variations. 22-24: Steep twills. 25: Undulating twill. 26: Birds eye. 27-28: Bird's eye variations. 29-30: Variations of rosepath. 31: Goose eye. 32: Straight 2/2 twill, color variations producing 33 and 34. 33: Houndstooth check, made of 4 D, 4 L repeat in warp and weft. 34: Guard's check, made of 2 D, 2 L repeat, same in warp and weft. 35: Simple twill pattern, color variations producing 36 and 37. 36: 4 midtone, 4 light warp repeat, with dark weft. 37: Light warp, 4 mid, 4 dark weft repeat. 38-39: A threading of 4 dark, 4 light, 4 mid, 4 light repeated in warp and weft produces a check pattern in plain weave (38) and a fancy check in 2/2 twill (39).*

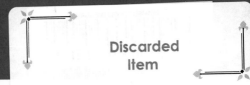